Extending Laura's Little House

A collection of extension activities to enhance the reading of selected writings of Laura Ingalls Wilder

By Lela Gunn
Illustrations by Emily Gunn

Extending Laura's Little House

A collection of extension activities to enhance the reading of selected writings of Laura Ingalls Wilder

Little House in the Big Woods - page 7

Little House on the Prairie - page 11

On the Banks of Plum Creek - page 17

By the Shores of Silver Lake - page 24

The Long Winter - page 29

Little Town on the Prairie - page 34

These Happy Golden Years - page 39

The First Four Years - page 43

By Lela Gunn
Illustrations by Emily Gunn

I have always enjoyed reading. I still have my first Bible and a few of my early readers. I have the Bible story book that my father read from at bed time when I was a little girl. I remember loving Marguerite Henry books and Laura Ingalls Wilder books as a young student. I remember my aunt taking me to the library and the treasures I would bring home. I remember falling in love with Janette Oke's books as a young wife and falling in love all over again with picture books when I became a mother.

In my home there is not room for another piece of furniture, or room for another knickknack on my shelves; but, there is always room for another good book. In my home you might find books stacked on a make shift side table, on a window ledge, in baskets and even on the floor. Of course I have book shelves, but they are all full. I joke with my friends that I have my pilots license. I pile books here and I pile them there. I love books.

It doesn't help that we home school. We study a wide variety of topics each year and of course, we need at least one good book on each subject. Yes, we have a public library, a very new and large public library. And yes, we have direct access at home to the internet; however, nothing compares to owning your own books, at least not in my book.

As previously stated, I love to read, but; it was not until I began work on my master's degree that I fell in love with the idea of extending children's literature. While pursuing my degree, I had a wonderful professor that truly loved children's literature. He introduced our class to wonderful books and to the idea of extending stories by using a variety of activities. As a young teacher I loved sharing such activities with my students and now as a home school mom; I love sharing such activities with my daughter.

What follows is a variety of activities that can be used to extend your reading of Laura Ingalls Wilder's Little House Series. Some books lend themselves to more activities than others. Please realize that what follows are suggested activities to enhance your reading of the Little House books. It is not necessary to try and do all of the activities. Just have fun and choose those activities that you feel will enhance your learning. (Please note that at this time, I have not included activities for the book Farmer Boy as I am most interested in following the continuity of Laura's life and Farmer Boy tells the story of Laura's husband, Almonzo's childhood.)

I suggest you keep a notebook of your activities with special divided sections for Animals, Birds, Christmas, Clothing, Fabric, Plants, Prices: Then and Now, Recipes, Handwriting, Transportation and Machinery, Vocabulary and Miscellaneous. (Pocket dividers are suggested. They work well to hold items waiting to be hole punched or waiting to be placed in page protectors.) You might wish to choose a notebook with pockets on the inside covers to hold work in progress. The internet will be a valuable tool in locating information. (Please note that while this collection of activities seems to be written to the student, it is strongly recommended that the parent play an active part in choosing activities.)

It is my hope that some of the activities I have suggested will be enjoyable to you and foster in you a love for extending literature.

Extension Activities for Little House in the Big Woods

Chapter one: Color the state of Wisconsin on the blank map of the United States. (A map is provided for you to copy at the end of the book.) Place this map in your notebook as you will be coloring in other states later.

Look up wolves, bears, wild cats, muskrats, mink, foxes and deer; these are the animals that lived near Laura and her family. Make notes about the animals or draw pictures of them for your notebook. Use animal reference books or the internet to find information.

Sample beef jerky.

Collect a basket full of the vegetables mentioned in this chapter: carrots, cabbage, beets, turnips, potatoes, red peppers, onions, pumpkin and squash. Display the basket for a few days and then use some of the vegetables for making dinner - maybe make vegetable soup. Place your recipe in your notebook.

Purchase an ear of feed corn and remove the kernels. Wrap the corn cob in a handkerchief and play with your own corn cob doll.

Chapter 2: Make your own butter by filling a clean plastic peanut butter jar about 1/3 full of cold heavy cream. (Any cream or even whole milk will work, but you get results quicker with heavy cream.) Add a couple of marbles for quicker results. Tighten the lid and begin shaking. When a lump forms in the jar, you have made butter. Remove the marbles. Pour off the remaining liquid, or drink it - it is butter milk. You may wish to salt your butter before enjoying it on bread or crackers.

Make paper dolls by drawing them on white card stock and cutting them out. Use colored pieces of card stock or patterned scrapbook papers to make clothes for your dolls. You might wish to keep your paper dolls in a pocket of your notebook.

Chapter 3: If you are lucky enough to know someone who has a muzzle loader, ask them to share with you how to clean and load the gun.

Find out about screech owls by researching in an animal book or on the internet. There are internet sites where you can hear owl sounds. Place a picture or sketch of a screech owl in your notebook.

Chapter 4: Check the internet or an old cookbook for a recipe for vinegar pie. Try baking one. To speed up the process try using a store bought crust. Remember to add the recipe to your notebook.

Remember the next time it snows to make a snow angel.

Compare Laura's Christmas in the big woods of Wisconsin to your family's Christmas celebrations. You could use a Venn diagram to accomplish this and keep the diagram in the Christmas section of your notebook.

Begin a book about Laura's Christmas gifts. You can add to it each time you read about Christmas time. Try making an accordion style book. You can add a new page for each Christmas. Keep this book in a pocket in your notebook.

Stick a large, red apple full of cloves and enjoy the scent.

Make pancake men like Ma did.

Chapter 5: Spend a Sunday afternoon (or any afternoon) doing only those things Laura was permitted to do on Sundays.

Compare Laura's birthday celebration to your last birthday. You may wish to write down your comparisons and keep them in the miscellaneous section of your notebook.

Sing *Pop Goes the Weasel*. Write the words in your best handwriting and add them to your notebook.

Chapter 6: Mend an article of clothing.

Visit a fabric store and look at all of the calico fabrics. Look for ones that may be similar to those Pa brought back for Ma and the girls. Mary's was a china-blue pattern on a white background, and Laura's was dark red with little golden-brown dots. Ma's calico dress was brown, with a big feathery white pattern all over it. If you find similar fabrics, you might wish to purchase a small amount and add a swatch to a piece of card stock for your notebook.

Chapter 7: Sample maple sugar candy. I have found this before at the general store in Cracker Barrel Restaurants.

Discuss maple sugaring time. There are many good reference books as well as internet articles on this topic.

Talk about Ma's delaine dress. (Delaine was a fine woolen or woolen and cotton fabric that resembled muslin.) Talk about your finest outfit and what makes it special.

Chapter 8:   Make hasty pudding. You can find a recipe on the internet. Place the recipe in your notebook.

Find pictures of vintage corsets and petticoats on the internet. Print pictures to place in your notebook. Talk about how you would feel if you had to wear these today.

Visit the fabric store once again and look for calico fabrics similar to the fabric of Laura's aunts' dresses. Aunt Docia wore a dress that was dark blue with sprigs of red flowers and green leaves all over it and Aunt Ruby wore a dress that was wine-colored and was covered all over with a feathery pattern in a lighter wine color. Can you find a fabric that might look like Ma's dress? Ma wore her dark green delaine, with little leaves that looked like strawberries scattered over it. Don't forget Grandma. Grandma wore a dark blue calico with autumn-colored leaves scattered over it.   If you find similar fabrics, consider purchasing small amounts and adding swatches to your notebook. Remember to label the swatches so you can remember who wore each dress.

Sing *Buffalo Gals*. You might like to add the words to this song to your notebook. Here is another chance to practice your best handwriting.

If you are brave and industrious, purchase some pure maple syrup and make your own maple sugar candy. You can find instructions on the internet. If you do this activity, be sure and include your instructions in your notebook.

Chapter 9: If possible visit a general store.

Have a picnic lunch of bread, butter and cheese, hard-boiled eggs and cookies.

Chapter 10:   This chapter deals with making cheese and gathering honey. You might want to try your hand at making cheese - there are many easy cheese recipes available on the internet. (Rennet is now synthesized and available in tablet form.)

Buy a piece of honey comb and sample fresh honey.

Sing the song about Old Grimes to the tune of *Auld Lang Syne*. You may like to add the words to this song to your notebook. Remember to use your best handwriting.

Chapter 11: Discuss the meaning of *crying wolf*. Do you think Charley deserved what happened to him?

Research yellow jackets. Use the internet or a book about animals. Draw a picture of a yellow jacket and write down a few facts about them. Add this information to your notebook.

Chapter 12: Talk about the threshing machine and the term *horse power*. List other inventions that have made life easier over the years. Put your list in the Transportation and Machinery section of your notebook.

Chapter 13: Sing *Old Susanna* and *Auld Lang Syne*. You might like to add the words to these songs to your notebook.

Extension Activities for Little House on the Prairie

Chapter 1: Using the map in your notebook draw in the Mississippi and Missouri Rivers and color in Minnesota, Iowa, Missouri and Kansas.

Look on the internet and either print or sketch a picture of a papoose for the miscellaneous section of your notebook.

Try bread and molasses.

This chapter reveals that Pet and Patty were mustangs. Read about mustangs in a book about horses. Add any interesting notes or sketches about mustangs to your notebook.

Chapter 2: Discuss the saying, *All's well that ends well.*

Look up the terms ford and bluff. Be sure to find a definition that matches the context of the word used in your reading. Add these words and definitions to the vocabulary section of your notebook.

Chapter 3: Try mixing cornmeal with a dash of salt and a bit of water. Pat the mixture into little cakes and fry them in a bit of oil in a frying pan. This is what Laura and her family ate on their journey.

Find a grocery that sells fat salt pork. Fry some and try some. (This may simply be called salt pork at the grocery.)

Look up the following animals: Wolf, lynx and coyote. Place a picture or sketch of each in your notebook. You may wish to write a few facts about each animal.

Chapter 4: Serve pancakes and bacon for breakfast. If the weather permits, eat outside and pretend you are Laura waking up on her journey.

Check out the internet or a book about birds and find pictures of the meadowlark and dicksissle. Later in this chapter you will encounter the phoebe and meadowlark. Draw and label these birds and place them in your notebook.

Look up pictures of a prairie gopher and sketch this animal for your notebook.

Look up the words pannikin and sadiron. Add these words and definitions to the vocabulary section of your notebook.

Chapter 5:   Locate the Verdigris River on a map of Kansas and mark the river on the map in your notebook.

Look up the word chink and add it to the vocabulary section of your notebook.
(If you build a cabin from pretzel rods, you can use icing to chink your cracks.)

Build a log cabin out of pretzel rods and icing. Pretzel rods can be cut carefully with a knife to allow shorter rods for the front and back of the cabin. You might want to make a doorway and attach a piece of fabric for the quilt at the door.

Ask your parents or grandparents if they know the tune to *I'm a Gypsy King* or *Old Dan Tucker*. If they do, have them teach it to you. Consider writing the words in your best handwriting and adding them to your notebook.

Research the nightingale and add a sketch to your notebook.

Chapter 6:   Continue working on your log cabin. Depending on how big your cabin is, you might add beds and a table.

Look up the word puncheon. Add this word and definition to the vocabulary section of your notebook. Remember Pa intends to make a puncheon floor for the cabin.

Chapter 7: If you did not research wolves during chapter one of *Little House in the Big Woods*, or earlier in this book, do so now. Be sure and add a picture or sketch to your notebook. How would you feel if you were Laura looking out the window openings at the wolves?

Laura's dog Jack is a bull dog. Find or sketch a picture of a bulldog for your notebook.

Chapter 8:   Serve fried mush for breakfast and if you are brave enough you might try making chicken hash. If you use recipes, include them in your notebook.

Chapter 9:   Laura used her knife and fork just as her Ma had taught her. Discuss the importance of good table manners.

See if you can find pictures of larkspur, goldenrod and daisies for your notebook.

Add sketches or pictures and descriptions of a wood pigeon and a brown thrush to your notebook.

If you have a creek nearby and the weather is nice, see if you can find a minnow. These can often be caught in a small net used for fish tanks.

Consider serving roast chicken for supper. If you used a recipe, place it in your notebook.

Chapter 10: Make or purchase a sun bonnet and wear it for a while. Do you agree with Laura that when you are wearing it, you can only see what is in front of you?

Discuss what Ma meant when she said that she did not like to be beholden, not even to the best neighbors. Are you beholden to anyone?

Read the last paragraph of the chapter and make your own drawing of Laura's new home. Place your drawing in the miscellaneous section of your notebook.

Chapter 11: Find an article or book about Plains Indians. Make a fact sheet for the miscellaneous section of your notebook.

Discuss the importance of being obedient even if you think it might be alright to do what you have been told not to do. (Remember Laura thought it might be alright to turn Jack loose when the Indian came.)

Chapter 12: Discuss the beds that pa made. Notice that the straw mattress was laid on rope.

Look up the term red work embroidery. Purchase a plain white pillow case, or make one from bleached muslin. Draw two little birds on the pillow case and outline them with red thread. (You can purchase pencils at a fabric store that you can use to draw your birds. These special pencil lines fade away when they get wet so only your embroidery will be seen.)

Look up the word windlass and add this definition to the vocabulary section of your notebook.

Talk about why Pa sent the candle down into the well before a person was allowed to enter the well. Do an experiment by putting a jar over a lighted candle. What happens to the candle when the oxygen is gone?

Chapter 13: Add sketches and facts to your notebook on both the whip-poor-will and long horned cattle.

Have you ever heard frogs croaking? If it is spring time, go to a pond or creek at dusk and listen to the croaking of the frogs. If it is not the right season, check the internet for a site that allows you to listen to frogs.

Chapter 14: Add pictures or sketches of ox-eyed daisies and sumac to your notebook.

Purchase some beads and string a necklace.

Discuss how Laura felt about giving her beads to Carrie. Have you ever felt this way?

Chapter 15: Make and enjoy a blackberry pie. Place your recipe in your notebook.

Add a sketch and information about blue jays to your notebook.

Research fever and ague (malaria.). Write a paragraph for the miscellaneous section of your notebook.

If the season permits, enjoy a watermelon.

Chapters 16: Using your best handwriting, copy the words to *Bye, Baby Bunting*. Place these words in your notebook. Ask your parents or grandparents if they know the tune and can sing it for you.

Look up the word quinine. Add this definition to the vocabulary section of your notebook. Why do you think that Laura's family might be needing more quinine?

Chapter 17: Mrs. Scott said that she did not know why the government made treaties with the Indians. Find the definition of treaty and put it in the vocabulary section of your notebook.

Chapter 18: Add pictures or sketches of beaver, muskrat and mink to your notebook.

Do a little research on the Osage Indians. Add your findings to the miscellaneous section of your notebook.

Do an internet search on Indian Territory. Find out what present day state was the area to which most Indians were moved by the late 1800's.

Chapter 19: Use some scraps of fabric and make a nine patch quilt block. (You may have calico left from what you purchased for some of the activities in *Little House in the Big Woods*.)

Remember that Laura's family is living along the Verdigris River. You have already marked this on your map. Now mark Independence, Missouri on your map. This is where Mr. Edwards encountered Santa Clause.

Purchase and enjoy a peppermint stick.

Make a batch of heart shaped sugar cookies.

Add the gifts Laura received this Christmas to your Christmas book.

Chapters 20: Learn to play Cat's Cradle with a piece of string. Go to the library and check out a book on string games. Cat's Cradle is a popular string game.

Learn to do a hand clapping game to the words of Bean Porridge Hot. Check the library for a book on hand clapping games for kids,

Find a recipe and make bean porridge. Be sure and put the recipe in your notebook.

Add a sketch or picture of a cougar to your notebook. This is most likely the animal that is referred to as a panther in this chapter.

Chapter 21: Play Hopscotch.

Eat little sour pickles.

Discuss why the Indians may have been having a jamboree. Look up the word jamboree and add it to the vocabulary section of your notebook.

Chapters 22: Look up the meaning of the word furrow. Add the definition to the vocabulary section of your notebook. Pa built a furrow to help control the fire. Find out if fire fighters use similar techniques today when fighting wild fires.

Do some research and find out what all parts of the buffalo were used by the Indians after a buffalo hunt.

Chapter 23: Define stockade and talk about why some of the settlers might have wanted to build one.

Chapter 24 and 25: Add sketches and facts about curlews, sandpipers, killdeer and mocking birds to your notebook. (You may already have information collected on the mocking bird.)

If the season is right, plant a small vegetable garden.

Discuss the phrase, *there is no great loss with out some small gain.*

Discuss why Laura's family has to leave their little house on the prairie.

Chapter 26: Laura's family decided in just one day that they must leave the prairie. They packed in one morning and were on their way. Discuss the following questions. Could your family move in such short notice? If you could only take what could fit in a wagon, what would you pack for the journey? Make a list and add it to the miscellaneous section of your notebook.

Sing *Old Susanna*. Add the words to you notebook. Remember to practice your best handwriting.

Extension Activities for On the Banks of Plum Creek

Chapters 1: Find a picture or make a sketch of a willow tree for your notebook.

Find a book about dug outs. Do a little research on this type of home. How does it differ from your home? Add your research to the miscellaneous section of your notebook.

Chapter 2: Look up morning glory in an encyclopedia or on the internet. If the season is right, plant some near your home. Draw a picture for your notebook.

Chapter 3: Find pictures or make sketches of blue flags and rushes for your notebook.

If possible visit a creek. Sit quietly and see if you can see any water bugs, dragon flies or small fish.

Walk barefoot through the mud and enjoy the feeling of it as it squishes between your toes.

Chapter 4: This would be a good time to discuss water safety.

Chapters 5: Find a picture of a badger in a book about animals. Sketch him and put your picture in your notebook. You might wish to add a few facts about the animal.

Laura had disobeyed and had to earn her father's trust. Write a paragraph about trust. You may want to look up the meaning of the word and add it to the vocabulary section of your notebook.

Chapters 6: Define lichen. Take a walk and see if you can find a rock covered with moss or lichen. Draw a picture of your findings and place it in your notebook.

Read a book or article about butterflies. What type of butterflies live in Minnesota? You may wish to add some sketches to your notebook.

Do you live near a farm, or country store that sells fresh cows milk. If possible, purchase some to sample.

On a world map, locate Sweden, Norway and Germany. These are the countries from which the Ingall's neighbors had migrated.

Chapter 7: Get up early and watch the sun rise and walk barefoot in the early morning dew. Do a bit of research and find out how dew forms.

Chapters 8: If you have not already done so, find out what a threshing machine does. Try and find a picture for the Transportation and Machinery section of your notebook.

Chapter 9: Purchase some fresh plums. Enjoy one raw and then look for a recipe using plums. Prepare the recipe and don't forget to include a copy of it in your notebook.

Visit a grocery store and see how many varieties of plums you can purchase and sample.

Chapter 10: In *Little House in the Big Woods*, Laura records that Ma wore her delaine dress to the sugaring dance at Grandma's. In this book, she records that Ma wore the beautiful challis that she had worn to the sugaring-dance at Grandma's. Define challis and compare the definition to the definition of delaine.

Talk about hoop skirts. Look for pictures in pattern books or on the internet. Add a picture of a hoop skirt to your notebook. (It is possible to purchase or make a hoop skirt.)

Chapter 11: If possible, purchase and try some horehound candy. You can even make the candy yourself if you are so inclined. (Horehound is an herb from the mint family that has a bitter apple-like flavor.) You may wish to find a picture of this herb for your notebook.

Chapters 12: Find a recipe and make parched corn or purchase a pack of corn nuts which is a variation of parched corn. If you make your own, don't forget to include the recipe in your notebook.

Copy the prayer, *Now I Lay Me Down to Sleep,* in your best handwriting. Include it in the miscellaneous section of your notebook.

Chapter 13: Gather some old buttons and make a button string necklace.

Add a page to your Christmas book. You might want to take a cupcake wrapper and glue it to the a page. In it you can placed 6 bits of colored paper to represent the Christmas candy. Fold the wrapper over the candy at the top, bottom and sides to represent the paper package. Don't forget to add the Christmas horses to your page.

Chapter 14 and 15: This is another good opportunity to talk about water safety.

Chapter 16: Add pictures or sketches of violets, buttercups, sorrel and lavender to your notebook.

Talk about the pros and cons of buying things on credit.

Try to acquire some wood shavings from pine boards. Play with them as Laura did.

Chapters 17: Define the word patent and add your definition to your notebook.

Compare Laura's new house to the cabin in Indian country and the dug out. What features does the new house have that your house has?

Find a box and keep your treasures in it. What will you put in your box?

Chapter 18: Find a picture or draw a sketch of a crab for your notebook. Also sketch a leech. Find out why doctors used to put leeches on sick people.

Chapter 19: Look in an animal book or on the internet for pictures of the fish that Pa caught in his fish trap. Pa caught buffalo fish, cat fish, shiners, pickerel and bullheads. You may want to sketch these fish for your notebook.

Chapter 20: Look up the following birds in a bird or animal book or on the internet. Add sketches or pictures of them to your notebook: Blue heron, prairie chicken and snipe.

Laura and Mary pass a black smith shop on their way to school. Find out what a blacksmith does. Consider writing a paragraph about blacksmiths and include it in the miscellaneous section of your notebook.

Chapter 21: Play Ring Around the Rosie and Uncle John is Sick in Bed.

Chapters 22: What is a velocipede? If possible, print a picture for the Transportation and Machinery section of your notebook.

You can find a picture of a jumping jack toy on the internet. You might even be able to make your own using heavy card stock and string.

Serve white cake and lemonade as a special treat.

Chapter 23: Make popovers which are sometimes referred to as vanity cakes. Simply mix 1 cup of milk with 2 beaten eggs. Next add 1 cup of flour and a pinch of salt. Fill greased muffin tins ¾ full of batter and bake at 425 for 20 minuets or until golden. These can be dusted with powdered sugar and enjoyed. Add the recipe to your notebook.

Chapter 24: Locate a church near you that has a belfry. Find out when they ring the bell and drop by and listen.

Talk about Pa's generosity in giving his $3.00 to help purchase the church bell.

Chapters 25: There are many internet articles about the grasshopper plagues of the 1800's. Search for an article and read more about what happened during this time.

Draw a diagram of the grasshopper: Label the head, thorax and abdomen. Add this drawing to your notebook.

Chapter 26: Pa has to walk about 200 miles to find work. Figure out a destination that is about 200 miles from your home and imagine walking from your home to that destination.

Chapter 27: Talk about how your summer clothes differ from Laura's.

Chapter 28: As it turned out, Pa had to walk 300 miles to find work. What destination is 300 miles from your house? Can you imagine having to walk that far?

Pa found work that paid a dollar a day. Find out how much your father is paid each day.

Chapter 29: Have you ever had to part with a favorite toy? Talk about how you felt. If you have not had to part with a favorite toy, what toy would you hate to part with? Would you feel as sad as Laura felt?

Chapters 30: Visit the fabric store again and search for golden brown flannel and dark blue flannel. Buy a small amount of each and cut swatches for your notebook. You might like to draw a picture of Laura and Mary and give them dresses cut from the flannel. Add this picture to your notebook.

Sing *When Johnny Comes Marching Home*. Find the words and add them to your notebook. Practice writing them in your best handwriting.

Chapter 31: Try making popcorn balls. Include your recipe in your notebook.

Buy a piece of fake fur and fashion a muff to keep your hands warm in the winter.

Add a page to your Christmas book. Be sure and include all of the gifts that Laura received.

Chapter 32: Find out more about grasshoppers. Do an internet search for grasshopper eggs or grasshopper facts. You might wish to add some of your findings to your notebook.

After reading this chapter, draw a picture that shows the grasshoppers walking.

Chapter 33: Find pictures or draw sketches of ragweed and tumbleweed (also called Russian thistle). Add your pictures to your notebook. Find out why tumbleweed has this name.

Tumbleweed spreads it's seeds as it tumbles. Find out how some other plants disperse their seeds. Plants to check out might include dandelions, maple trees and the cockelburr.

Think about your neighbors. Are they as willing to help you as Mr. Nelson was to help the Ingalls family? Are you willing to help them? What does the Bible say about neighbors? (Isaiah 41:6, Mark 12:31)

Chapter 34: Try boiled, mashed or creamed turnips. Include the recipe you used in your notebook.

Is there an event coming up that you are counting the days till it arrives? Try Mary's method of counting the days. Make a mark on a piece of paper for each day until your event. Erase one mark each day. When the marks have all been erased, it is time for your big event.

Chapters 35: Define blizzard. Talk about the worst snow storm you can remember.

Chapter 36: Find directions on the internet or in a book on quilt making for making a bear claw quilt block. Use some fabric scraps to try and make this block. If you have not yet made a 9 patch block, try it instead as it is much easier to construct.

Using your best handwriting, copy the hymn that Laura's family sang. The words are at the end of the chapter.

Chapter 37: Define the word pendulum. Add this to the vocabulary section of your notebook. Do you have a clock with a pendulum? If not, try to find a picture of one.

Discuss why you think that Ma put a lighted lamp in the window.

Play Bean-Porridge hot or another hand clapping game. You might be able to find the words to various hand clapping games on the internet or in a library book. See how fast you can play before making a mistake.

Chapter 38: Serve cornmeal mush for breakfast. Is this like the hasty pudding Grandma made in the big woods of Wisconsin?

Gather your family and play pussy-in-the-corner. You can probably figure out the rules as you read about Laura playing the game with Ma, Mary and Carrie.

Practice telling the story that Ma told. Put your drawing of the bird in your notebook.

Chapter 39: If you did not learn how to play the string game Cat's Cradle in *Little House on the Prairie*, learn how to play it now. You can find a book of string games at the Library.

Chapter 40: Buy a box of oyster crackers and enjoy them as a snack.

If you are very brave, try making oyster stew. If you make this, include the recipe in your notebook.

Chapter 41: Serve baked beans and corn bread for supper.

In your best handwriting, copy the words to *Captain Jinks of the Horse Marines* and place them in your notebook.

Extension Activities for By the Shores of Silver Lake

Chapters 1: Do a bit of research to find out the symptoms of scarlet fever. Define scarlet fever in the vocabulary section of your notebook.

Pa takes a job paying $50.00 a month. Make a list of things your family does each month that costs more than $50.00. (buy groceries, pay the electric bill...) Put your list in your notebook under Prices: Then and Now.

Chapter 2: Color North and South Dakota on your map. At this time in history, North and South Dakota were not states. They made up the Dakota Territory.

Find an encyclopedia article on the Dakota Territory. This is the area to which the Ingall's family will be moving.

Chapter 3: If you have enjoyed your visits to the fabric store, go once again and look for calico similar to what Laura and Mary wore on the train. Laura's dress was a brown calico sprinkled with small red flowers and Mary's was gray calico with sprays of blue flowers. Add swatches of these fabrics to your notebook.

Find out what year Laura was born. She is now almost 13. What year would it be now? Find out what year train travel began and find out what year the first continental railroad was completed. Record this information in the Transportation and Machinery section of your notebook.

Chapters 4: Comment on some of the things that Laura was experiencing for the first time: Train travel, running water, the roller towel...

Discuss how the meal Laura ate at the hotel differs from eating at a restaurant today.

Ma and the girls waited for Pa in the parlor. Define the word parlor and add your definition to the vocabulary section of your notebook.

Chapter 5: Serve bread and butter and hard boiled eggs for lunch. Don't forget the salt and pepper for dipping.

Do you have a tent? If the weather cooperates, sleep outdoors on a blanket. If you cannot sleep outside, pitch the tent indoors and still sleep on a blanket.

Chapter 6: Find a definition for whiffletree and add it to the vocabulary section of your notebook.

Lizzie was married at age 13. Find out how old your parents, grandparents and even great-grandparents were when they were married.

Discuss the difference between trotting and galloping. Draw a picture of Laura riding the black pony.

Chapters 7: Locate the Big Sioux River on a map of South Dakota and draw it onto the map in your notebook.

Read the description of Big Jerry and make a sketch of him for your notebook.

Chapter 8: Define slough and add this definition to the vocabulary section of your notebook.

Laura mentions the Big Slough. A slough is like a swampy area. She also mentions wild ducks, geese, herons, cranes and pelicans feeding among the grasses. Add sketches of these birds to your notebook. (You may have already sketched a heron.)

Find pictures of buffalo beans and tiger lilies to sketch for your notebook.

If the season permits, find a place to collect a bouquet of wild flowers.

Chapters 9: Try making fried mashed potato cakes by shaping cold mashed potatoes into pancake shapes and frying them in a bit of oil.

Before going to bed, try brushing your hair 100 strokes.

Chapter 10: Look up the meaning of boisterous. Add this definition to your notebook.

If the building of the railroad is of special interest to you, try locating a book with pictures of this time in history. Do any of the pictures in your book look like the things Laura described in her writings?

Chapters 11: Find out how your father gets paid. Does he get paid right up to yesterday, or does he have to wait like the railroad workers waited ?

Ask someone to help you figure out the meaning of *discretion is the better part of valor*. Use the dictionary if necessary.

Chapter 12: Find a book about ducks at the library, or do an internet search. Try and find pictures or make sketches of the mallard, bluebill, canvasback and teal duck for your notebook.

Find out the wing span of a swan. Add a sketch or picture of a swan to your notebook.

Chapter 13: Talk about how you might feel if your family had to spend the winter alone with the nearest neighbor 60 miles away. Use a map to figure out a place that is 60 miles away from your home. That is how far away Laura's nearest neighbor lived.

Chapters 14: Serve canned peaches for dessert today.

Use your best handwriting to copy the stanza of Pa's song that begins: Then love your neighbor as yourself. Place this in your notebook.

Chapter 15: Find out what the disease consumption is called today. Describe this disease on paper and add the paper to the miscellaneous section of your notebook.

Locate some waltz music and instructions for learning this type of dance.

Chapter 16: Enjoy a game of checkers.

Chapters 17: If you live near an ice skating rink, or if it is winter outside, plan to go ice skating.

Chapter 18: Find a picture of wolf tracks to include in the animal section of you notebook.

Chapter 19: Hem a square of white muslin and make a hankie like the girls made Ma for Christmas.

Learn to knit. (It is easier than you might think.)

Reminisce about your favorite Christmases.

Sing *Jingle Bells* even if it is not Christmastime.

Chapter 20: Find a picture of a horse drawn bob sled for the Transportation and Machinery section of you notebook.

Find a recipe and stir up a batch of biscuits. Be sure and put the recipe in your notebook.

Chapter 21: Record Laura's Christmas gifts in your Christmas book.

If cooking is something you enjoy, try making a sour dough starter and later sour dough biscuits.

Make an apple pie. (You might even try drying apple slices then rehydrate some and use them for your pie.)

Try making popcorn the old fashioned way, in a pan on the stove.

Chapters 22: Do you have any biscuits left? If so, try some hot with honey.

Using your best handwriting, copy the words to: *She can make a cherry pie, Billy boy, Billy boy.* Place this in your notebook.

Read about the Homestead Act of 1862. How many acres were settlers allowed to claim?

Chapter 23: Define the word repined and add the definition to the vocabulary section of your notebook.

Find De Smet, South Dakota on a map and mark it on the map in your notebook.

Chapter 24: Figure out how much you might spend if you were traveling and needed lodging and a meal. How much did Pa and Ma charge? Place this information in your notebook under Prices: Then and Now.

Chapter 25: Find out about homesteading in the 1880's. Write a paragraph to place in your notebook.

Chapter 26: Discuss how hard Ma and Laura worked to make $42.50?

Find a recipe and make sage or onion stuffing. You might try both types and decide which is your favorite. Remember to put the recipes you use in your notebook.

Chapter 27: Draw a picture of what Laura and her sisters might have looked like the morning that they woke up in a snow drift.

Look up the words diligence and perseverance and add these definitions to the vocabulary section of your notebook.

Chapter 28: Copy the first stanza of the song Laura's family sang in their new home. Use your best handwriting and put your finished work in your notebook.

Chapter 29: Add pictures or sketches of wild onion and wild crocus to your notebook.

Find a picture of a cottonwood tree. Sketch it and find out how the cottonwood tree got it's name. Add your sketch to your notebook.

Discuss how Laura must have felt when they could not find Grace.

Chapter 30: Add a sketch or picture of violets to your notebook.

Do a quick study on buffalo. Find out why they nearly became extinct in the 1800's. Add information about buffalo to your notebook. Include a picture or a sketch.

Chapters 31 and 32: Copy the words to the song that Pa sings at the end of the book. Use your best handwriting. Consider framing this and hanging it in your home. If you choose not to frame your work, add it to your notebook.

Extension Activities for the Long Winter

Chapter 1: Add sketches or pictures of a dragon fly, prairie hawk and garter snake to your notebook.

Define haycock. Add this definition to the vocabulary section of your notebook.

Make some ginger water by squeezing the juice of a lemon (Ma used vinegar) into a quart of cool water. Add one tablespoon of freshly grated ginger root wrapped in cheesecloth. Shake well before drinking. Sweeten with sugar to your liking.

Chapter 2: Talk about safety and the importance of staying on a trail when walking.

Gather some information on the Morgan horse. Include your findings in your notebook along with a picture or a sketch.

Chapters 3: If the season is right, try making green tomato pickles or green tomato relish.

If you happen to be reading this book in the late summer or early fall, try your hand at making a green pumpkin pie like Ma did.

Chapter 4: Make cambric tea, a drink for children, made from hot water, milk, sugar and a small amount of strongly brewed tea.

Serve hot baked beans and hot tea for supper.

Chapter 5: Add a picture or sketch of the great auk to the animal section of your notebook.

Chapters 6 and 7: Use a Bible concordance to find scriptures that mention the wings of a bird. Which scripture do you think Laura was referring to when she said that she wished she had the wings of a bird?

Chapters 8 and 9: Find a picture of black button up shoes to put in your notebook. (Search the internet for Victorian black button shoes.)

Memorize the 23 Psalm.

Do you think Laura was glad that Ma made her wear her red flannels ?

Make and serve hot ginger tea. Here is an easy recipe. Be sure to add it to your notebook. You will need 4 cups of water and a 2 inch piece of fresh ginger root. Peel the ginger root and slice it into thin slices. Bring the water to a boil in a saucepan. Once it is boiling, add the ginger. Cover it and reduce the heat to a simmer. Simmer for 15-20 minutes. Strain the tea. Add honey or sugar and lemon to taste.

Chapters 10: Make and enjoy buck wheat pancakes. Try them with molasses like Almonzo did. Place a copy of the recipe in your notebook.

Chapter 11: Find a picture of a railroad hand cart for the Transportation and Machinery section of your notebook.

Sing *We Will Roll the Old Chariot Along*. Copy the words of one verse using your best handwriting and place the words in your notebook.

Chapter 12: Learn to knit or crochet. It doesn't take too much practice to make something simple like a dish cloth.

Sing a course of *The Old Gray Mare She ain't What She Used to be*.

Chapters 13: Find a definition for the word parboil and add it to the vocabulary section of your notebook.

Have a memory verse contest and see who can quote the most Bible verses.

Copy the words to *Jesus is a Rock in a Weary Land* in your best handwriting and add them to your notebook.

Chapter 14: Enjoy toast with cherry preserves.

Serve baked potatoes with butter and hot biscuits with butter for dinner today.

Chapter 15: Try making a small braided rug. You can even make a very small one and use it as a coaster for a mug.

Chapters 16:   Hand write a letter to a friend or relative who lives far away.

Chapter 17:   Discuss how Laura must feel as she realizes that her family is running out of needed supplies. Do you think that Mary is feeling the same way?

Chapter 18: Find an easy picture to cross stitch. You might choose counted cross stitch, as easy kits are readily available at most fabric stores.

Do an internet search on hair receivers and find out what this Victorian item was used for. You might want to print a picture for the miscellaneous section of you notebook.

If you have not already tried oyster stew, now would be a good time to try it.

Remember to add Laura's gift this Christmas to your Christmas book.

Chapters 19-20: Purchase some hay at a feed store or from a local farmer. Try making some hay sticks. If you are successful, you might try burning them to see how long they will last. The tighter you twist, the longer they will burn.

Follow Ma's directions for making a button lamp. You can use vegetable shortening in place of the axle grease.   With permission, light it in the sink in case you need to put it out quickly.

Chapter 20:   Add a sketch or drawing of the prong horned antelope to the animal section of your notebook.

Chapters 21:   Serve roast beef and gravy for supper. Think about how you would feel if you knew that you had no other food but a few potatoes and some wheat to bake bread.

Add the definitions of patience and perseverance to your notebook.

Chapter 22 and 23:   Laura said that the Fifth Reader was full of beautiful speeches and poems. Have your mother help you choose a speech or poem to memorize and recite for your family.

Pa suggests that they read for awhile about Livingstone's Africa. Find out who David Livingstone was and what he did in Africa.

Define saleratus. Add the definition to your notebook.

Chapter 24: Take this opportunity to do a study in nutrition. Talk about the food groups and how each benefit's the body. Discuss whether the Ingall's family is getting enough nutrition. Laura mentions feeling numb and half-asleep and refers to Carrie as looking thin and white, could this be the result of poor nutrition?

Try making codfish gravy. There are several recipes available on the internet. Include this recipe in your notebook.

Chapter 25: What is a tintype? Do a bit of research on this type of photography.

Discuss the sayings: *Be sure you're right, then go ahead* and *better be safe than sorry.*

Chapter 26: Enjoy a game of checkers or cards.

Chapter 27: Add a sketch or picture of a buckskin horse to your notebook. You may wish to include a paragraph about the buckskin horse in your notebook.

Chapters 28: If you can acquire some wheat and have access to a coffee grinder (even an electric one), try grinding some wheat and making some bread. You may have to use a yeast recipe if you do not have any sour dough starter.

Using your best handwriting, copy the words to the song: *Great is the Lord and Greatly to be Praised*. Place this in your notebook.

Add the definition of chilblained to your notebook.

Chapter 29: Define palaver and add this definition to your notebook.

Do a little research on frostbite. Read about the symptoms and how it is treated.

Chapter 30: Try eating only coarse wheat bread for a meal.

Define chinook (make sure you define it as a type of wind). Add this definition to your notebook.

Read Daniel 4:33 to understand why Pa called Carrie Nebuchadnezzar when she asked if they could eat grass.

Chapters 31: Find out what a fascinator is. Remember there was one in the Christmas barrel for Mary. You might want to print a picture and description for the miscellaneous section of you notebook.

Chapter 32 and 33: Regardless of the time of year, serve a Christmas dinner. Have turkey, stuffing, potatoes, cranberry jelly, apple pies and even a sugar frosted loaf cake.

Use your best handwriting to copy the final course of the song that is sung after Laura's Christmas dinner in May. Place your finished paper in your notebook.

Extension Activities for Little Town on the Prairie

Chapters 1-2: Try to find a picture of a breaking plow for the Transportation and Machinery section of your notebook.

If you have not already done so, add sketches or pictures of violets, buttercups and sheep sorrel to your notebook.

You may have already memorized the 23rd Psalm. If so, review it and if not, consider committing this Psalm to memory. You might like to make a neat handwritten copy of the Psalm for your notebook.

Find some information on the angleworm and include your information and a sketch in your notebook.

If the season is right, plant a garden. Even a small container garden can be nice. If it is not the right time for planting, try placing a couple of lima beans on a wet paper towel. Place the beans and towel in a zip lock baggie and watch the beans sprout.

Chapters 3: Add a picture of a striped gopher to your notebook. Is this animal different from the prairie gopher that was mentioned in *Little House on the Prairie*?

Research kittens. Find out how old they are when their eyes open and how old they should be before they are taken from their mother. What color is a blue kitten?

Chapter 4: Every week Pa was earning $15. Compare this to what your Pa earns in one week. You might want to include this information in the Prices: Then and Now section of your notebook.

It is unlikely that you will be able to sample a roasted pig's tail, but you might enjoy trying pork rinds which are purchased in the snack food aisle of most grocery stores and are the fried skin of a pig.

Chapter 5: Find a picture of an early sewing machine to add to your notebook.

Visit a fabric store and locate bolts of muslin, calico, flannels and silks. Are you able to find lawns, challis and cashmere? If possible, purchase small swatches for your notebook. It is possible that you have swatches of most of these fabrics already. Be sure to label the fabrics when you add them to your notebook.

Practice some hand sewing; baste a seam, sew on a button or even try making a button hole by hand.

Chapters 6-7: Laura had earned $9.00 in 6 weeks. Find out how much someone you know gets paid for one hour of work and compare this to Laura's wages. Place your findings in the Prices: Then and Now section of your notebook.

Chapter 8: Read about Fort Ticonderoga.

Memorize a portion of the Declaration of Independence. You may wish to copy what you have memorized for your notebook. Remember to use your best handwriting.

Enjoy a glass of fresh squeezed lemonade. Find a recipe and include it in your notebook.

Chapter 9: Use the internet or an old pattern book (sometimes fabric stores give away the old ones and most have a historic section) to find pictures of hoop skirts, petticoats, union suits and corsets. You may wish to add these pictures to your notebook.

Look up Godey's Lady's Book on the internet. You might enjoy seeing some of the pictures of early fashions.

Look up the definitions for saucy and modulate. Add these definitions to the vocabulary section of your notebook. Remember that Ma used both of these words when talking to Laura about her voice.

Research the types of blackbirds that are found in South Dakota. Be sure to include the yellow headed blackbird and red winged blackbird. Add pictures or sketches to you notebook.

Pa plans on selling the heifer calf for $15.00. How much would a heifer calf sell for today. Put this information in your notebook under Prices: Then and Now.

Chapters 10: Spend a full day helping your mother clean the house. Imagine how tired Laura and Carrie must have been with out all of our modern conveniences.

Locate Vinton, Iowa in an atlas and mark this town on the map in your notebook.

Make an autograph album out of card stock and ask your friends to sign it. Keep this in a pocket of your notebook.

Chapter 11: Do an internet search to find a picture of a polonaise dress. You may also wish to do a search to find out about a jabot. Pictures or sketches can be added to the clothing section of your notebook.

Chapter 12: Look up the word gilded. Add the definition to your notebook. Are there any books in your house with a gilded cover?

Read a poem by Tennyson. *The Flower* and *Flower in the Crannied Wall* are both good choices and can both be found on the internet. You may wish to copy a Tennyson poem in your best handwriting for your notebook.

Chapters 13: Learn to make tassels from red embroidery floss. Remember Almonzo's horses had red tassels hanging from their bridles.

Chapter 14: Discuss Miss Wilder's unfair actions toward Carrie and Laura.

Chapter 15: Read and discuss Matthew 23:25-25 and Luke 11:39. Why do you think Laura is reminded of these verses in chapter 15 ?

Define nubia and place the definition in your notebook.

Copy the verse Ma wrote in Laura's autograph album into your own album. It is good advice for everyone.

Chapters 16: You might choose to copy some of the verses the girls exchanged in their autograph albums. Use your best handwriting and place you finished work in your notebook.

Use card stock to design your own name cards. This can be done on the computer, with rubber stamps or free hand.

Chapter 17: Find a picture of a princess style dress for your notebook.

Talk about how Laura used her pencil like a curling iron and called her bangs a lunatic fringe.

Chapter 18: Assemble your family and have your own spelling match.

Chapters 19: Play a game of charades.

Have your own debate on Who was the Greater Man: Washington or Lincoln?

Add Laura's Christmas gift to a page to your Christmas book.

Do a bit of research on Braille. See if you can write your name using the Braille alphabet. Place this in the miscellaneous section of your notebook.

Chapters 20: Enjoy fresh oranges with white frosted cake. You might even try peeling the orange to look like a flower the way that Mrs. Woodworth peeled them.

Play Drop the Hankie or Blind Man's Bluff.

Chapter 21: Do a bit of research on the minstrel show. Write a paragraph for your notebook. Place it in the miscellaneous section.

Chapters 22-23: How does your family celebrate the 4th of July? Remember Laura stayed home from the town celebration to watch Grace and study the Constitution.

Take a look at the Constitution. Consider memorizing the preamble.

Have you ever attended a revival meeting? There is usually a time of singing. Copy one of the songs that Laura sang at the revival meeting. Use your best handwriting and place your work in your notebook.

Chapter 24: Consider having a school exhibition for your extended family. Include some mental arithmetic, recitations and sentence diagrams as well as American history. This would be a great time to recite the Preamble to the Constitution.

Find a picture of a horse drawn cutter and add the picture to the Transportation and Machinery section of your notebook.

Chapter 25: Take a 12 mile drive. Twelve miles was the distance from Laura's home to the school she would be teaching. She would not be able to come home each evening. Discuss how long this drive might take when traveling by horse and buggy.

Laura would be making $40.00 teaching school for 2 months. Compare this to the salary of a beginning teacher today.

Extension Activities for These Happy Golden Years

Chapters 1: Discuss the importance of thinking before you speak.

If you were going to be away from home for 2 months, what would you pack for your journey? Notice the basic contents of Laura's satchel.

Chapter 2: Do a bit of research on one room school houses. You can either search on the internet or make a trip to the library.

Chapter 3: Smile at everyone you meet today and think about Laura's words that it *takes two to make a smile*.

Chapter 4: Look up the words to the *Doxology*. You can find them in a hymn book or on the internet. (The first line is: *Praise God from whom all blessings flow*.) Use your best handwriting to copy the words for your notebook.

Spend a Sunday afternoon the way Laura did; enjoy reading and letter writing.

Chapters 5-6: Discuss the meaning behind some of the expressions used in Laura's writings; expressions such as *bump on a log, least said, soonest mended* and *wise as a serpent and gentle as a dove*.

Chapter 7: Put yourself in Laura's place, how would you feel if you were the one staying with the Brewster family?

Chapters 8-9: Do an internet search to see how cold winters get in your area. Remember it was 40 degrees below zero one Friday when Almonzo went to get Laura and take her home.

Chapters 10-12: If it is winter, try and arrange to take a sleigh ride. If it is not winter, make a note to do so when winter comes.

Try writing your own composition on ambition. Place your composition in the miscellaneous section of your notebook.

Chapters 13-14: Do a bit of research on the Bad Lands and the Black Hills of South Dakota. If possible, add pictures or sketches of these places to your notebook.

Chapters 15: Try your hand at beading. Bead a ring or bracelet or try making a lamp mat like Mary brought home for Ma. Coil and stitch a circle of cotton rope then add strings of brightly colored beads around it.

Chapter 16: Add a picture or sketch of the prairie rose to your notebook. The wild prairie rose is the state flower of North Dakota.

Robert Herrick wrote the poem that Mary quoted to Laura on their Sunday walk. The poem begins: Gather ye rosebuds, while ye may... Find this poem on the internet and copy all or part of it into your notebook. Be sure to use your best handwriting.

Chapters 17: Add Laura's Christmas present to your Christmas book.

Chapter 18: Laura will be making $25 a month teaching school. Find out how much a beginning teacher makes in your area and compare this to what Laura is making. Add this information to the Prices: Then and Now section of your notebook.

Chapter 19: See if you can locate brown poplin, brown cambric and brown silk at the fabric store. Consider adding swatches of these fabrics to your notebook.

Find a picture of a poke bonnet and add the picture or a sketch to your notebook.

Discuss what Ma meant when she told Laura to remember that *pretty is as pretty does*.

If you have not already done so, locate pictures of a buggy and a cutter for your notebook. These can be filed under the Transportation and Machinery section of your notebook. Note the differences in the two types of transportation.

Chapters 20: Add a picture or sketch of a choke cherry bush to your notebook.

Chapter 21: Bake a pie plant (rhubarb) pie. Place your recipe in your notebook.

Write a paragraph about how your family celebrates the 4th of July and how your celebration differs from Laura's family's celebration.

Chapter 22: Practice singing scales: Do, Re, Mi, Fa, Sol, La, Ti, Do.

Chapters 23: Sing Three Blind Mice. Try singing this in a round with at least two other people.

Copy the Anthem *The Heaven's Declare the Glory* into your notebook. Use your best handwriting.

Chapter 24-25: Make popcorn balls.

Trace Almonzo's journey on your map.

Add Laura's Christmas present to your Christmas book.

Chapters 26-28: Define grippe. Add this definition to the vocabulary section of your notebook.

Visit the fabric store once again. Look at muslin. Compare the bleached muslin to unbleached muslin. Why do you think Laura purchased the bleached variety?

While at the fabric store, look for fabric similar to what Laura may have chosen for her dresses. She chose a delicate pink lawn with small flowers and small green leaves scattered all over it. (Lawn is a fine, sheer cotton fabric with a tight plain weave and drapes nicely.)

Chapters 29: Do a bit of research on tornadoes and define the word cyclone. Add your findings to your notebook.

Chapter 30: Add pictures or sketches of the following trees to your notebook: box elder, willow and maple. You might wish to add sketches of their leaves. If you have not already added a picture of the cottonwood tree, you might choose to include it as well. These are the trees that Almonzo planted on his tree claim.

Chapters 31: When Laura suggested a new way to sew the fabric together to make sheets, Ma said that their grandmothers would *turn in their graves*. Discuss the meaning of this phrase and suggest some things that we do today that might make our grandmothers *turn in their graves*.

Do an internet search or find a book at the library that shows Victorian clothing, especially undergarments. Sketch pictures of a chemise and drawers.

Consider yet another outing to the fabric store to purchase a swatch of black cashmere. Cashmere is a soft woolen fabric made from goat's wool. Add a swatch of fabric to your notebook.

Chapter 32:   Locate a book on quilt blocks at the library, or do an internet search, try to find *a dove in the window* quilt block. If you are interested in sewing, try piecing your own *dove in the window* block. You may have enough scraps from your previous trips to the fabric store to piece your quilt block. If you do not wish to actually piece this quilt block, you might still sketch it for your notebook.

Make a big white cake and serve it for dinner. Try a recipe that requires you to beat the egg whites until stiff. Remember that Laura would not have had an electric mixer to help her with this task. Include your recipe in your notebook.

Search for wedding pictures from the late 1800's. Search on the internet, in flea markets or among your own family belongings. Notice how many brides are dressed in black. (If you have any *Little House* resource books, some show pictures of Laura in her black cashmere dress.)

Compare more recent family wedding pictures to the pictures you found from the 1800's.

Discuss how Laura and Almanzo's wedding was different from most modern day weddings.

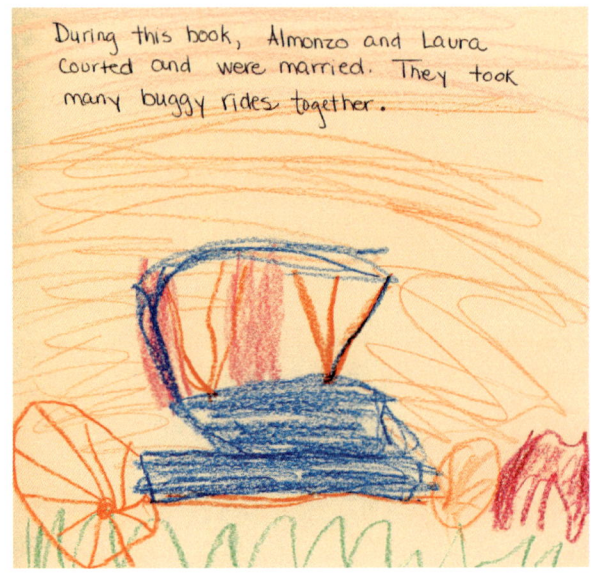

Extension Activities for the First Four Years

Chapter 1: Discuss the saying, *everything is evened up in this world. The rich have their ice in the summer but the poor get theirs in the winter.* What do you think this means?

Add a sketch of a geranium to your notebook. If the season if right, purchase a plant and enjoy it's beauty.

Do a bit of research on the sulky or riding plow. Discuss how this makes life easier for farmers. If possible, add a picture to the Transportation and Machinery section of your notebook.

Cook a pot of navy beans for supper. Remember to soak them the night before. Serve them with hot corn bread. Did you use a recipe? If so, place it in your notebook.

If possible, go horse back riding. Imagine that you are Laura riding Trixie.

Read Proverbs 22:7. What does the Bible say about borrowing? How does Laura seem to feel about borrowing?

Laura bought a bay colt. Find out what the term bay means in reference to her colt.

Research geese and find out why they fly in a V formation.

Be sure and add Laura and Manly's Christmas gift to your Christmas book.

Find out what the term chattel mortgage means.

Manly suggests making homemade ice cream after the hail storm; but Laura doesn't feel like celebrating. Do you feel like celebrating? If so, make homemade ice cream. Discuss why Manly was suggesting they make ice cream. Was he being resourceful?

Chapter 2: Manly sold 30 tons of hay at $4 a ton. This made his yearly crop income $120.00. Can you find out how much hay costs today? Record you finding under Prices: Then and Now in your notebook.

Do you remember why Laura chose to name her baby Rose? Rose weighed 8 pounds. Find out how much you weighed when you were born and ask if there were special reasons why your name was chosen.

Laura and Manly sold two 2 year old steers for $12 each. The $24.00 was used to buy groceries. Find out how much a 2 year old steer would cost today. How many groceries can be purchased for $24.00? Record your findings under Prices: Then and Now in your notebook.

Chapter 3: Do a bit of research on the disease diphtheria. What are the symptoms? Is it prevalent today? Place your findings in the miscellaneous section of your notebook.

Look up Shropshire Sheep. Write a paragraph on the breed and make a sketch for your notebook.

Laura sold her 3 year old colt for $100 and bought Shropshire sheep for $2 each. Find out how much would these animals sell for today. Record your findings under Prices: Then and Now in your notebook.

Chapter 4: Find out about Durham oxen and include a sketch and description in your notebook.

Manly pays $25 each for 2 oxen. How much would an ox cost today? Place this information under Prices: Then and Now in your notebook.

Take a moment and find a bit of information on the author Sir Walter Scott. Scott wrote novels as well as poetry. Although many of his poems are long and some difficult to understand, you may wish to include one of his poems in the miscellaneous section of your notebook.

The wool from the Wilder's Shropshire sheep sold for 25 cents a pound. Compare this to today's prices. It may be helpful to know that the Wilder's sheared an average of 10 pounds of wool per sheep. Place your findings in the Prices: Then and Now section of your notebook.

Discuss Ma's saying, *We'll always be farmers, for what is bred in the bone will come out in the flesh.*

In your best handwriting, write the saying that was on Laura's bread plate: *Give us this day our daily bread.* This plate is on display at the Laura Ingalls Wilder Home Association in Mansfield Missouri. This can be placed in the miscellaneous section of your notebook.

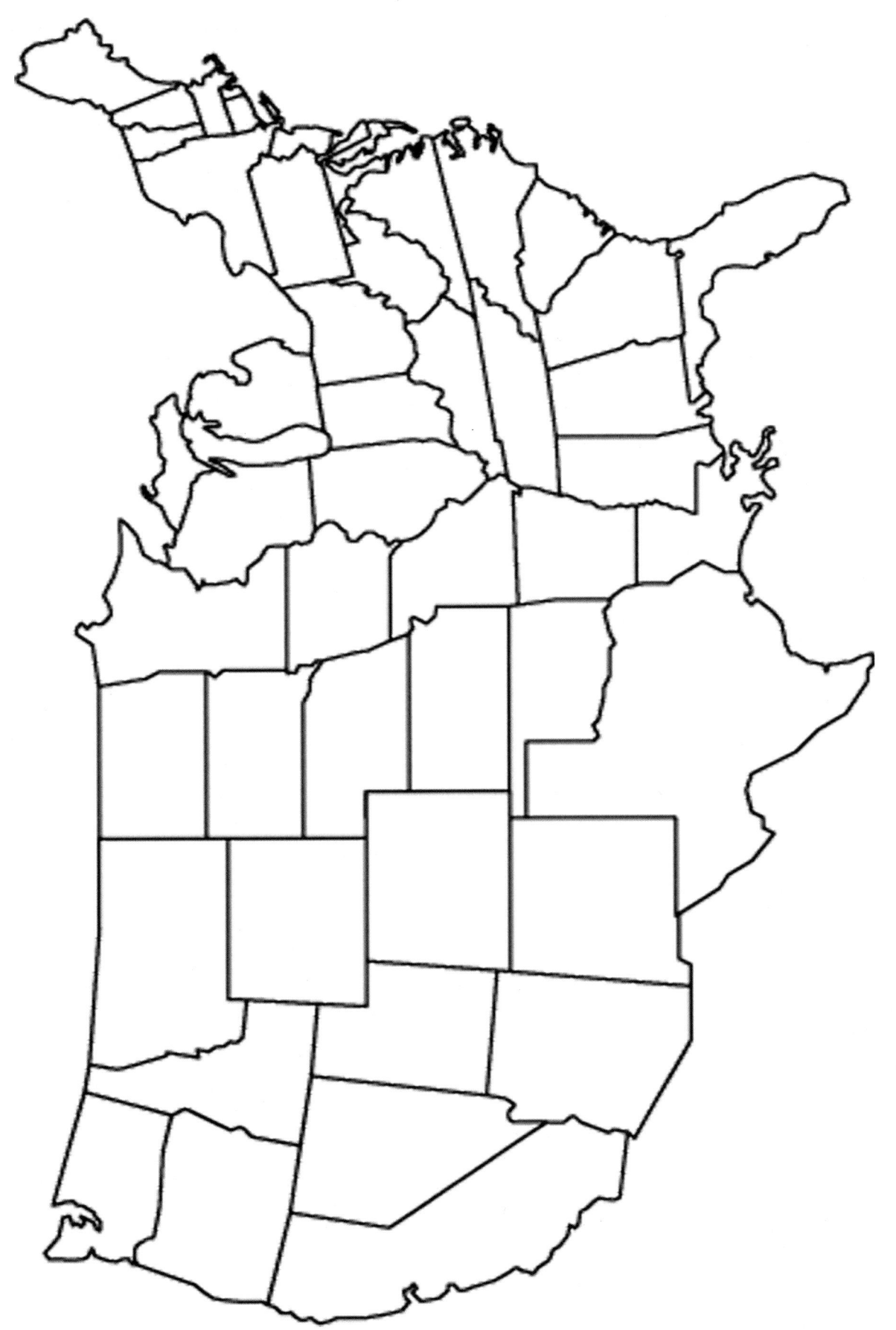

It is my hope that you have enjoyed extending Laura's Little House and that you now have a better understanding of the time period in which Laura lived. I hope that you have enjoyed compiling your notebook and have gained useful knowledge from the activities you completed.

Made in the USA
Columbia, SC
30 August 2020